100
ROADSIDE WILDFLOWERS
OF SOUTHWEST WOODLANDS

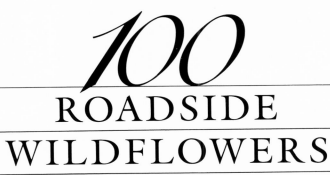

100
ROADSIDE
WILDFLOWERS

OF SOUTHWEST WOODLANDS

Janice Emily Bowers

SOUTHWEST PARKS AND MONUMENTS ASSOCIATION
TUCSON, ARIZONA

©Copyright 1987 by Southwest Parks and Monuments Association
ISBN 0-911408-73-8
Library of Congress Number 87-060531

Editorial: T.J. Priehs
Design: Christina Watkins
Production: Nancy Curtis, Christina Watkins
Lithography: Lorraine Press, Inc., Salt Lake City, Utah

All photographs by Steven P. McLaughlin and Janice Emily
Bowers except as credited.

Cover photograph: *Castilleja* sp. (George H.H. Huey)

THE SETTING

Exactly what makes a woodland? It's not the density of the trees, because woodland trees can be so thick that it's impossible to walk in a straight line for more than two or three yards, or so sparse that you can hardly throw a rock from one tree to the next. A woodland is generally defined by the height of the trees – usually more than fifteen feet and less than sixty. This eliminates such large forest trees as Douglas-fir and ponderosa pine, leaving the many species of oaks, pinyons and junipers.

In the Southwest, we recognize two broad types of woodland. In southern Arizona and southern New Mexico (and also in the Mexican highlands of Sonora and Chihuahua) various species of oak, pine and juniper characterize the woodland. Among them are Emory oak, silverleaf oak, gray oak, Arizona oak, Chihuahua pine, Mexican pinyon and alligator-bark juniper. In northern Arizona, northern New Mexico, Nevada, Utah and Colorado, most oaks drop out of the woodland, and pinyons and junipers are the dominant trees. Single-needle pinyon and Utah juniper are particularly widespread and abundant in this more northern woodland.

Deserts, of course, are known for their paucity of rainfall, just as forests are known for being wet. Woodlands fall between these two extremes. Yearly precipitation in Southwest woodlands ranges from about twelve to twenty inches – somewhat more than the maximum of ten or so inches received by the desert and somewhat less than the thirty or more inches that fall at high elevations in the mountains. In the Southwest, woodlands have a winter and a summer wet season: winter precipitation includes some snow as well as rain; summer rainfall comes mostly as drenching thunderstorms.

The Southwest can be broadly defined to include the area from southeastern California to the Oklahoma panhandle and west Texas. For this book, I have employed a narrower definition and consider the Southwest to be simply Arizona and New Mexico. Wildflowers, however, don't recognize state boundaries, and many of the plants depicted herein can be found in the adjacent states of California, Utah, Nevada, Texas, Colorado, Sonora and Chihuahua.

For ease of reference, the flowers in this book have been arranged by color. To learn about related species, look for plants having the same family name.

THE WOODLAND IN BLOOM

The diversity of woodland wildflowers is astonishing. The hundred wildflowers presented in this book could have been multiplied several times without exhausting all the possibilities. Southwest woodlands are particularly fortunate in their location, for they get a double dose of wildflowers from the Rocky Mountains and from the highlands of Mexico.

People familiar with the Midwest and East have learned to expect a procession of wildflowers throughout the growing season. In the Southwest, the wildflower parade is less orderly. Some species bloom only in June or only in September, but most parade in cycles, blooming in spring and again in summer. The trigger that sets them off is moisture: in the spring, it is the moisture stored in the soil from winter rain and snow, and in the summer, it is the regular thunderstorms that start in July and continue into September.

Still, the major blooming season of Southwest woodlands is the summer. Luckily for wildflower lovers, summer lasts a long time in southwestern woodlands, long past the time when the first snows have fallen in the northern United States. As late as November, you can still find members of the Sunflower Family in bloom – the sunflowers, the rabbitbrushes and the goldeneyes turn entire hillsides as golden as the autumn foliage at higher elevations.

Most wildflowers in Southwest woodlands are perennials. Unlike annuals, which must grow from seed every year, perennials survive from one year to the next. Certain perennials die back to the ground after they have dispersed their seeds. Their roots remain in the soil, waiting to send up leafy stems and flower buds when warmer temperatures arrive in spring and summer.

FLOWER VISITORS

While you're looking at woodland wildflowers, you'll probably enjoy watching the animals that visit them. The main purpose of flowers is to attract insects and other visitors which pollinate the flowers by transferring pollen from the anthers of one flower to the stigmas of another. Most plants prefer cross-pollination; that is, movement of pollen between plants. In fact, many will not set seed if the pollen is transferred between flowers on the same plant. Self-pollination is usually not to the long-term advantage of a plant.

Many of the flower visitors you'll notice will be bees of one sort or another. No doubt you'll recognize the familiar honeybee; the stout, black carpenter bee; and the black and yellow bumblebee; but others might be unfamiliar. Almost all bees in the Southwest are solitary; instead of living in colonies as honeybees do, they live singly. Solitary bees make their nests in tunnels in logs or soil. They lay a few eggs in special cells inside each tunnel, providing pollen for the larvae to eat once the eggs hatch. Much of this pollen comes from wildflowers, and in fact solitary bees are the most important pollinators of woodland plants. Moths are also important pollinators, particularly the large sphinx moths sometimes called hawkmoths. These stout-bodied moths hover as they feed from flowers after dark. Unlike bees, which visit flowers for pollen, nectar and, rarely, oil, moths come only for nectar. Other flower visitors you might see include a variety of butterflies, beetles, wasps, flies, ants, hummingbirds and bats. Not every visitor is useful to the flower: some simply rob pollen or nectar without pollinating the flower in return. Many flowers have evolved structures that minimize theft. You'll learn about some of these adaptations in this book.

A WORD ABOUT PLANT NAMES

Although common names can be delightfully descriptive and informative, they are entirely unstandardized. Most plants lack widely accepted common names. A few, however, have several, and to add to the confusion, some quite different plants even share the same common name. Fortunately, every plant has only one valid scientific name, which is shared by no other plant. Although scientific names are an essential tool for botanists, they can be a stumbling block for amateur wildflower enthusiasts. This need not be. Many people are afraid to pronounce the cumbersome Latin or Greek names, not realizing that they already know and use dozens of scientific names. Geranium, chrysanthemum, phlox, poinsettia, zinnia: all are scientific names. Moreover, not all botanists pronounce the Latin or Greek names the same way, and if they aren't in perfect accord, why should anyone else worry about it?

Scientific names come in three parts. The first part, the genus name, corresponds roughly to your family name. The second part, the species name, corresponds to your first name. Just as your first name distinguishes you from the other members of your immediate family, so a plant's species name distinguishes it from every other species in the genus. The third part of every plant name is the authority – the surname of the botanist who first described the plant as a new species. If a later botanist decides the plant belongs to a different genus, as sometimes occurs, his or her name becomes part of the authority, too. Often these surnames are abbreviated. Few botanists bother to memorize the authorities of every plant they know, and you don't need to worry about it either except to realize that the authority is part of the complete scientific name. The scientific names used in this book incorporate the most recent changes in nomenclature. Some may differ from those you already know.

Parts of a Flower

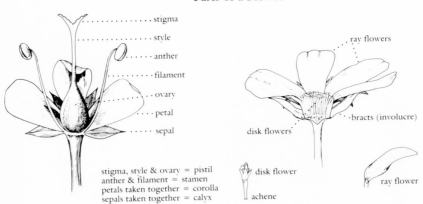

stigma
style
anther
filament
ovary
petal
sepal

ray flowers
bracts (involucre)
disk flowers
disk flower
achene
ray flower

stigma, style & ovary = pistil
anther & filament = stamen
petals taken together = corolla
sepals taken together = calyx

CONSERVATION

It's important to know that many plants in the Southwest are protected by law and may not be cut or dug up. All cacti, yuccas and agaves are protected, as are all the wildflowers that grow from bulbs. In national parks and monuments, all plants are protected. Remember, no plant will thrive in your hands the way it will thrive in its native soil.

1·BEARGRASS

The inconspicuous flowers of beargrass are borne in dense panicles three to five feet tall. Its leaves are harvested in Mexico for commercial broom production and have been used in basketry by the Tohono O'odham (Papago Indians) for centuries. The Indians dried the leaves in the sun for several days, then split them into narrow strands. The split leaves were then coiled into baskets, the successive coils being secured with a wrapping of yucca fiber. Beargrass is most abundant in desert grassland, where it quickly recovers from occasional fires by sprouting from the woody stem-base. It grows from western Texas to Arizona and northern Mexico.

Nolina microcarpa Wats.
Agave Family

2·SOTOL

If you find a disintegrating sotol plant, you'll see why it's also called desert spoon: the base of each slender leaf is wide and cupped like the bowl of a spoon. The sharply toothed leaves are very tough, and native peoples of the Southwest used sotol fibers extensively for cordage, baskets and sandals. The Tohono O'odham (Papago Indians) made sotol mats for drying fruits, leaves and roots. In the Sierra Madre of central Mexico, bootleggers distill a powerful alcoholic drink – called sotol – from the succulent crowns of the plants. The large, black bees known as carpenter bees make their nests inside the old stems of sotol, yucca and agave. Sotol grows in desert grassland and oak woodland from southern Arizona to western Texas and northern Mexico. Its inconspicuous flowers appear in May and June.

Dasylirion wheeleri Wats.
Agave Family

3·NARROWLEAVED YUCCA

George H.H. Huey

Like all yuccas, narrowleaved yucca is pollinated exclusively by female moths of the genus *Tegeticula*. The moth collects pollen from the anthers and rolls it into a ball, then lays her eggs inside the small, green ovary of a yucca flower on another plant. After she has deposited her eggs, usually no more than one egg for every row of seeds, she rubs the ball of pollen into the stigma of the yucca flower, thus ensuring that fertile seeds will develop as food for her offspring. Just as the yucca depends solely on the *Tegeticula* moth for pollination, so the moth caterpillars rely exclusively on yucca seeds for food. Neither one could exist without the other. Although the yucca loses a few seeds to the developing caterpillars, sufficient seeds remain to perpetuate the species. Narrowleaved yucca blooms in May and June and can be found in sandy places in New Mexico, Arizona and Utah.

Yucca angustissima Engelm.
Agave Family

4·DATIL

Datil, one of about a dozen yuccas in the Southwest, was a kind of general store for many native peoples in the region. Probably ninety percent of all the twisted cord made by southwestern Indians came from yucca fiber, much of it from datil. These fibers are the stiff, curling strands along the edges of the tough, narrow leaves. Indians also wove the fibers into sandals, mats, nets and baskets. The dried roots of datil were soaked in water to produce lather for shampooing and washing. Indians competed with birds, deer and insects for the large, sweet, fleshy fruits that ripen in the summer. The fruits were eaten raw or were cooked to a thick paste which was dried and later added to water to make a sweet drink. Datil, also called banana yucca after the fruits, blooms from April to July. It occurs in Colorado, Utah, Nevada, Arizona, New Mexico, Texas and California.

Yucca baccata Torr.
Agave Family

Charles T. Mason, Jr.

5·ANTELOPE HORNS

Milkweeds have been used medicinally for centuries. In fact, the genus *Asclepias* is named after Asklepios, the Greek god of medicine. In ancient times, worshippers of Asklepios slept in his temples in the belief that the god would prescribe medical remedies in dreams. In parts of New Mexico, antelope horns is known as *inmortal* and is used for congested lungs and to ease childbirth. The plants probably contain cardiac glycosides, a class of compounds that act upon the heart. (Like many medicines, cardiac glycosides can be toxic if used incorrectly.) Since milkweed sap also contains asclepain, an enzyme similar to the papain used in meat tenderizers, there might be a chemical basis for the folk remedy of rubbing the milky juice on warts to make them disappear. In the Southwest, antelope horns grows on rocky slopes in desert grassland and in openings in oak woodland. It occurs from Kansas and Arkansas to Nevada, Arizona and northern Mexico.

Asclepias asperula (Decne.) Woodson
Milkweed Family

6·HORSETAIL MILKWEED

A common weed of roadsides, pastures and ditches, horsetail milkweed occurs from Kansas and Colorado to Texas, Arizona and northern Mexico. Flowers of horsetail milkweed are borne in loose clusters. Each flower has an inner circle of tiny, upright sacks – the hoods – and an outer circle of triangular petals. Milkweed pollen comes in small, teardrop-shaped packets called pollinia. You might be able to remove a pair of pollinia by carefully inserting a needle between two hoods. Pollinia are highly specialized so that they clip onto the feet or legs of insects that visit the flowers, then unclip when the insect visits another milkweed flower. Every milkweed seed bears a tuft of fine, silky hairs that floats in the wind, thus dispersing the seed. During the Second World War, scientists used milkweed fluff as a substitute for kapok in life preservers. The hairs are hollow, making them excellent insulators and remarkably buoyant. Horsetail milkweed, like many milkweeds, is poisonous to livestock due to the glycosides in the milky sap.

Asclepias subverticillata (Gray) Vail
Milkweed Family

7·BROADLEAF MILKWEED

Broadleaf milkweed, with wide, cabbagelike leaves that clasp the thick stems, is easy to recognize. Like many other milkweeds, broadleaf milkweed contains a milky sap rich in cardiac glycosides, a class of compounds that act upon the heart. Too large a dose of cardiac glycosides can be fatal to livestock and humans. Surprisingly, caterpillars of the monarch butterfly thrive on milkweed foliage. The poisons they eat make them poisonous to predators – mainly birds. Even as adult butterflies, monarchs are full of the toxins ingested as caterpillars, and birds learn to avoid them. Broadleaf milkweed grows along roadsides and in pastures from Nebraska to Utah, Texas and Arizona. It blooms in spring and summer.

Asclepias latifolia (Torr.) Raf.
Milkweed Family

Charles T. Mason, Jr.

8·FALSE TOADFLAX

You probably know that a parasite is a plant that robs its host of water, nutrients and sugar. False toadflax is a hemiparasite: like a parasite, it attaches itself to the roots of a host plant, robbing it of water and minerals, but, as a green-leaved plant, it manufactures its own food. About two weeks after false toadflax seeds germinate, the seedlings attach themselves to the roots of a host plant by means of special conducting tubes called haustoria.

Through these haustoria, water and nutrients pass from host to parasite. Over 200 different species of plants are known to serve as hosts to false toadflax; in the Southwest, oaks are the most frequent host. False toadflax occurs throughout North America and flowers in the spring.

Comandra umbellata (L.) Nutt.
 ssp. *pallida* (A. DC.) Piehl
Sandalwood Family

9·LONG-FLOWERED FOUR O'CLOCK

Easily overlooked during the day, long-flowered four o'clock springs to life at dusk as the pure white flowers unfold, revealing long, purple filaments and orange anthers. A few species of hawkmoths with extremely long tongues are the only pollinators of the flowers, which, like many moth-pollinated blossoms, are pale, tubular, night-blooming and sweet-scented. Basically a tropical plant, long-flowered four o'clock loves warm, wet summers and dies back to the ground every winter. Long-flowered four o'clock occurs from west Texas, New Mexico and Arizona far south into Mexico.

Mirabilis longiflora L.
Four O'Clock Family

10·CLAMMYWEED

The stems of the aptly named clammyweed are quite sticky – even moist – due to their innumerable gland-tipped hairs. The exact function of these hairs is unknown. Some biologists have suggested that sticky hairs keep ants from crawling up stems to rob flowers of nectar. Clammyweed can be abundant on roadbanks, in washes and on disturbed sites. Like many native weeds, it has a wide distribution and occurs from Saskatchewan to British Columbia and south to Texas, New Mexico and Arizona.

Polanisia dodecandra (L.) DC.
ssp. *trachysperma* (Torr. & Gray) Iltis
Caper Family

Charles T. Mason, Jr.

11·CLIFF FENDLERBUSH

This shrub blooms in the spring on rocky slopes and canyon rims from Colorado to Texas and Arizona. Cliff fendlerbush was named after Augustus Fendler, a German who came to the United States in 1836. Asa Gray, the great American botanist, sent Fendler to collect in New Mexico, then little known botanically. Fendler collected over 17,000 specimens in the vicinity of Santa Fe, hoping to sell them to museums as a way of recouping his expenses. Unfortunately, he returned poorer by $200 and disillusioned with Asa Gray, who had disregarded heartfelt requests for financial assistance. Perhaps feeling guilty, Gray eventually named *Fendlera* in Fendler's honor, saying that Fendler had made excellent collections under much hardship.

Fendlera rupicola Gray
Saxifrage Family

12·UTAH SERVICEBERRY

Birds, squirrels, chipmunks, beavers and bears avidly consume the fruits of Utah serviceberry, a large shrub. The fruits, called pomes, look like miniature apples and are one of several fruit types in the Rose Family. Pomes (apples are typical pomes) are fleshy and tasty, with a few inedible seeds embedded in the flesh. In general, animals that eat pomes pass the seeds unharmed through their digestive tracts, thus dispersing the seeds. Utah serviceberry fruits ripen in June and July when little other wild food is available, making them particularly attractive to wildlife. The white, five-petaled flowers appear in April and May. Utah serviceberry grows from Colorado to Nevada, New Mexico and northern Arizona.

Amelanchier utahensis Koehne
Rose Family

John Richardson

13·FERN BUSH

Fern bush gets its name from its feathery leaves. Fragrant flowers give the plant the alternate common name of desert sweet. Borne in clusters at the stem tips, the small, white flowers are typical Rose Family blossoms, featuring five petals, five sepals, five pistils and numerous stamens. The dry seed pods represent a type of fruit known as a follicle. Other fruit types in the Rose Family include the plumed achenes of cliff rose, the apple like pomes of Utah serviceberry, and the fleshy drupes of cultivated pears and plums. Fern bush grows from eastern California to Oregon, Wyoming and Arizona.

Chamaebatiaria millefolium (Torr.) Maxim
Rose Family

John Richardson

14·APACHE PLUME

Apache plume, a shrub about three to five feet tall, thrives in disturbed spots such as roadsides and washes. Its large, white flowers appear from spring to fall and eventually produce pinkish, plumed fruits. Technically the fruit of Apache plume is an achene, a dry, one-seeded fruit that does not split open when ripe. Achenes may be winged, like elm seeds, or covered by a hard shell, like sunflower seeds, or attached to delicate plumes, as in Apache plume and several other members of the Rose Family. Apache plume can be found from southern Colorado and western Texas to southeastern California and northern Mexico.

Fallugia paradoxa (D. Don) Endl.
Rose Family

Stephen Trimble

15·CLIFF ROSE

The beautiful cliff rose, a large shrub or small tree of rocky slopes and woodland openings, blooms intermittently from spring to fall. The Navajo say that if cliff rose blooms in October, the winter will bring deep snow. So intensely fragrant are the flowers you can smell them from some distance away. Cliff rose fruits, like those of Apache plume, are plumed achenes, each derived from a single pistil. You can tell cliff rose from Apache plume in several ways. Cliff rose flowers are smaller (about half an inch across instead of an inch or more) and creamier in color. Cliff rose bears only several white plumes per flower, whereas Apache plume bears many pinkish ones. Also, Cliff rose bark is reddish, that of Apache plume light gray or white. Cliff rose occurs from southern Colorado to southeastern California and south to central Mexico.

Cowania mexicana D. Don
Rose Family

16·FERN ACACIA

The petals of fern acacia are less noticeable than the numerous white stamens. Each spherical flower head comprises many small flowers. Together they attract a variety of insects, including butterflies; singly, they'd probably be ignored. The pretty flowers appear in the summer rainy season. Fern acacia grows every year from perennial roots and dies to the ground after the first hard frost. It occurs across the southern United States and south into Central America.

Acacia angustissima (Mill) Kuntze
Pea Family

17·FENDLER BUCKBRUSH

Wasps, bees and butterflies often abound on the flowers of Fendler buckbrush. Indeed, you can sometimes locate the plants by sound before you see them. A thorny shrub usually less than four feet tall, Fendler buckbrush thrives on burned-over slopes in woodland and forest and is also common along roads and trails. Similar species include deerbrush (*Ceanothus integerrimus* Hook. & Arn.) which lacks spines and has green rather than gray leaves, and Gregg buckbrush (*Ceanothus greggii* Gray), which has leaves arising in pairs rather than singly along the stem. All three are valued honey plants, and all are browsed by deer. Fendler buckbrush occurs from Colorado and Utah to west Texas and Arizona. It blooms intermittently from spring to fall.

Ceanothus fendleri Gray
Buckthorn Family

18·WILD COTTON

Wild cotton, a shrub about five feet tall, bears white, cup-shaped flowers in the summer. Its scientific name, *Gossypium thurberi*, commemorates George Thurber, a former pharmacist who discovered wild cotton in Sonora in 1851. In those days, medicinal plants were as important as drugs prepared in the laboratory, and pharmacists were by necessity botanists. It's not surprising, then, that Thurber's pharmaceutical career eventually developed into the pursuit of botany. When Thurber served as botanist on the U.S. and Mexico boundary survey from 1850 to 1853, he made a large collection of southwestern plants. Wild cotton can be abundant on rocky slopes and in washes in southern Arizona and northern Mexico.

Gossypium thurberi Todaro
Mallow Family

Charles T. Mason, Jr.

19·PALE EVENING PRIMROSE

Fragrant white flowers that open at night and wilt by day often attract moths as pollinators. The blossoms of pale evening primrose fit this description exactly. As a hawkmoth hovers before the flowers, its fuzzy body picks up strands of pollen from the anthers. When the moth moves to the next flower, some of the pollen adheres to the sticky stigmas. Pale evening primrose grows in sandy soils and on dry hills across much of the West. It blooms from spring to fall.

Oenothera pallida Lindl.
Evening Primrose Family

20·TUFTED EVENING PRIMROSE

Larry Ulrich

The four large petals of all the evening primroses sit not on stems but atop a slender floral tube, which contains nectar. In tufted evening primrose, these tubes are quite long – up to four inches in one variety – and only long-tongued hawkmoths can reach the nectar. The moths pollinate the flowers as they move from one blossom to the next. Each tufted evening primrose flower offers about thirty-five microliters of nectar, no more than five or six drops of fluid. Although this seems to be a very small amount, it supplies about forty-two calories of energy to a moth, which itself expends only eleven calories of energy each minute in hovering and flying. Thus a moth can live quite well off a cluster of tufted evening primrose plants. Blooming from spring to summer, tufted evening primrose can be found at roadsides and on rocky slopes throughout the West.

Oenothera caespitosa Nutt.
Evening Primrose Family

George H.H. Huey

21·PRINGLE MANZANITA

Like the peach, the pear and the plum, manzanita is named after its fruit: *manzanita* is Spanish for little apple. A shrub from four to ten feet tall, Pringle manzanita sometimes forms inpenetrable thickets. The small, white to pinkish, bell-shaped flowers bloom in the spring and occasionally again in the summer. Manzanita is a major component of chaparral in California, where more than forty species challenge even the expert botanist. In the Southwest, only three species – Pringle manzanita, point-leaf manzanita (*Arctostaphylos pungens* H.B.K.) and green-leaf manzanita (*Arctostaphylos patula* Greene) – are abundant. Pringle manzanita occurs in Arizona, southern California and Baja California.

Arctostaphylos pringlei Parry
Heath Family

22·ARIZONA MADRONE

Arizona madrone is one of the most beautiful trees in the Southwest. You'll recognize it by the smooth, red bark; the glossy leaves; and the small, white, bell-shaped flowers. Arizona madrone is related to manzanita, also known for its smooth, red bark. The genus *Arbutus* is an ancient one. About fifteen million years ago, ancestors of Arizona madrone grew near Spokane, Washington, with gingko, incense cedar, redwood, swamp cypress, oak, magnolia and many other plants indicative of a warm, wet climate. Today, Arizona madrone grows in dense woodland with evergreen oaks and pines in southeastern Arizona, southwestern New Mexico and northern Mexico.

Arbutus arizonica (Gray) Sarg.
Heath Family

23·BEE BALM

Like many flowers, bee balm attempts to prevent self-pollination. The two anthers in a bee balm flower open and shed their pollen a day or so before the stigmas are receptive to pollen. Thus, a bee visiting the anthers of one plant will usually not be able to fertilize the stigmas on that plant, but will have to fly to an individual with receptive stigmas. If no bees visit the flowers, bee balm will resort to self-pollination as the receptive stigmas curl upwards into the pollen exposed in the anthers. Crushed bee balm leaves smell similar to oregano or marjoram. The fragrance comes from volatile oils in the foliage. Under a hand lens, these oil glands are visible as translucent, golden dots on the leaves and flowers. Bee balm blooms in the summer and grows along roadsides and in other disturbed spots from New Mexico and Arizona to northern Mexico.

Monarda citriodora Cerv.
  ssp. *austromontana* (Epling) Scora
Mint Family

24·SACRED DATURA

Sprawling plants of sacred datura are a familiar sight along Southwest roadsides in the spring and summer. The extravagant, white flowers, tinged with lavender on the margins, open around dusk and close by midmorning of the following day. Hawkmoths with long tongues are the major pollinators of sacred datura. The moths become intoxicated from drinking the nectar, and like vaudeville drunks, they stagger and weave from one flower to the next. Perhaps observation of the moths taught native peoples of the Southwest that they could use various parts of the datura as an hallucinogen. Although moths apparently suffer no permanent damage from the hallucinogenic alkaloids found in all parts of the plants, children have died after sucking datura flowers, and people trying to imitate Indian ways have poisoned themselves, sometimes fatally. Sacred datura occurs from Colorado to Texas, Arizona, southern California and Mexico.

Datura meteloides DC.
Potato Family

25·WRIGHT BEEFLOWER

A perennial herb that blooms in the fall, Wright beeflower can be abundant on rocky slopes. The tall, wandlike stems branch widely near the top, bearing many white-flowered heads. Wright beeflower was named after Charles Wright, who discovered it in northern Sonora in September 1851. A graduate of Yale, Wright taught and surveyed as the opportunity arose and collected plants wherever he went. As one of the Topographical Engineers assigned to the U.S. and Mexico boundary survey, he made a large collection of plants, adding much to the botanical knowledge of the Southwest. Wright beeflower occurs in Arizona, southern New Mexico, southern California and Sonora.

Hymenothrix wrightii Gray
Sunflower Family

26·NEW MEXICO FLEABANE

New Mexico fleabane, a common woodland wildflower, occurs in New Mexico and Arizona. Its pinnatifid leaves set it apart from all other southwestern fleabanes but one, the mountain fleabane (*Erigeron oreophilus* Greenm.). (Pinnatifid means deeply cut into narrow lobes.) The main difference between New Mexico fleabane and mountain fleabane is the presence of sticky hairs on the stems of the latter and their absence on the former. Because of their delicate white rays and yellow centers, fleabanes are sometimes called wild daisies.

Erigeron neomexicanus Gray
Sunflower Family

27·PALMER AGAVE

Stewart Aitchison

Instead of being thin and flexible, like the leaves of an elm, agave leaves are stiff and succulent and armed along the margins and at the tip with sturdy spines. Waxes that coat each leaf help prevent water loss. Like other so-called century plants, Palmer agave lives much less than 100 years. After eight to twenty years, the cluster of leaves sends up the only flowering stalk it will ever produce. Once fruits have been set, the entire plant dies. Though hummingbirds and insects visit the flowers, bats – attracted by the musky odor, profuse nectar and nocturnal blooming – are the most important pollinators of Palmer agave. In southern Arizona, nectar-feeding bats forage in flocks at agaves, circling above a plant and taking turns to swoop down to the flowers. After a few turns, each bat's head and shoulders are bright yellow from pollen. Palmer agave blooms in June and July. It is common on rocky slopes in New Mexico, Arizona and Sonora.

Agave palmeri Engelm.
Agave Family

28·SHINDAGGER

Few issues in biology are cut and dried, as the example of shindagger shows. Some years ago, several biologists put some bats and flowering stalks of shindagger into a cage, then watched as the bats lapped up the nectar from the small, yellow flowers and incidentally pollinated the blossoms. Other biologists have since objected that, unless confined with bats in cages, shindagger flowers are pollinated not by bats but by large bees such as bumblebees and the big, black carpenter bees. The yellow flowers are sweetly scented during the day, which is what we would expect in a bee-pollinated flower. (Most bat-pollinated flowers emit a musky fragrance at night.) Shindagger blooms on rocky slopes in May. It occurs in New Mexico, Arizona and northern Sonora.

Agave schottii Engelm.
Agave Family

Stephen Trimble

29·SULPHUR-FLOWER

About 120 species of wild buckwheat occur throughout the Southwest. The wild buckwheats thrive in a variety of habitats, from sheer cliffs to sand dunes to volcanic cinders. Both white-and yellow-flowered species can be found in Southwest woodlands. The name sulphur-flower is applied to several species of closely related, yellow-flowered buckwheats that grow with pinyons and junipers in northern Arizona, New Mexico, Utah and Colorado. *Eriogonum umbellatum* Torr. is perhaps the most common of these. Individual sulphur-flowers are tiny, but if you look closely, you can see that each consists of six nearly identical parts. Since there is so little difference between the three petals and three sepals, botanists often refer to them collectively as "tepals."

Eriogonum spp.
Buckwheat Family

Larry Ulrich

30·YELLOW COLUMBINE

Each of the five petals of columbine is prolonged into a narrow tube called a spur, a kind of nectar canteen. Many creatures visit the flowers of yellow columbine, among them hummingbirds, bees and hawkmoths, but only the hawkmoths have tongues long enough to reach the nectar inside the two-and-three-quarter-inch-long spurs. As a hawkmoth hovers at the blossom, its body touches the anthers and picks up pollen grains which it carries to the stigma of the next flower it visits. The red columbine (*Aquilegia triternata* Payson) has much shorter spurs and is pollinated by hummingbirds. Yellow columbine blooms throughout the summer and thrives in streambeds, springs, waterfalls and seeps. It occurs from southern Colorado to New Mexico, Arizona and northern Mexico.

Aquilegia chrysantha Gray
Crowfoot Family

31·WESTERN WALLFLOWER

Over most of its range, western wallflower is yellow, but in some locations the blossoms are orange or maroon. The petals are large for a member of the Crucifer Family, large enough that you can easily see the crosslike arrangement of petals that gives the family its name. (In Latin, Cruciferae means "cross-bearing.") Its long, narrow pods and tall stems will help you distinguish western wallflower from bladderpod [*Lesquerella gordoni* (Gray) Wats.], a desert wildflower that has small, globose pods and sprawling stems. Western wallflower can be common on shaded banks and in meadows from Saskatchewan to Washington and south to New Mexico, Arizona and California.

Erysimum asperrum (Nutt.) DC.
Crucifer Family

Peter Kresan

32·PRINCE'S PLUME

Larry Ulrich

The yellow-flowered stalks of prince's plume are a familiar sight on mesas and slopes in the pinyon-juniper woodlands. Prince's plume takes up the mineral selenium from the soil. Because selenium is similar in its chemical properties to sulphur, the plant simply substitutes selenium for sulphur in the production of amino acids, the building blocks of protein crucial to all living creatures. Although prince's plume can utilize selenium in place of sulphur, mammals cannot, and large amounts of selenium are toxic to livestock and humans. One or another of the several varieties of prince's plume can be found from southern California to North Dakota, southern Idaho and west Texas.

Stanleya pinnata (Pursh) Britton
Crucifer Family

Currants and gooseberries are easily recognized by their succulent berries and clustered, geranium-shaped leaves. The gooseberries generally bear bristly fruits, the currants smooth. Both are relished by wildlife, particularly ground squirrels, chipmunks and songbirds. Animals eat the fruits and pass the seeds unharmed through their digestive tracts, thus spreading the seeds from place to place. Golden currant (*Ribes aureum* Pursh) bears yellow flowers in the spring and grows at streamsides in woodlands and forests throughout the West. Orange gooseberry, which has reddish flowers and prickly, purple berries, is the most abundant gooseberry in southern Arizona. It usually grows with pines, as its scientific name – *Ribes pinetorum* Greene – implies. In northern Arizona, the wax currant (*Ribes cereum* Dougl.), which has white to pinkish flowers, is commonly found on shaded banks and along streambeds.

Ribes spp.
Saxifrage Family

33·WILD CURRANT

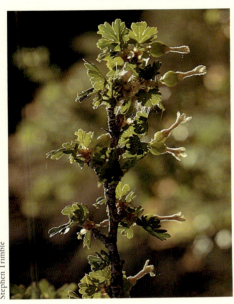

Stephen Trimble

34·LONGPOD SENNA

The five-petaled flowers of longpod senna bear two different sizes of stamens: a cluster of small, so-called "feeding" stamens in the center, and two larger "fertilizing" stamens projecting below. This arrangement facilitates pollination. As a bee collects pollen from the conspicuous feeding anthers, the inconspicuous fertilizing ones dust the bee with pollen. Unlike most anthers, which split longitudinally, those of longpod senna open by pores in the tips, and bees can remove pollen only by shaking the anthers. To do so, a bee wraps its body around an anther and vibrates its flight muscles, thus buzzing the pollen out of the apical pores. A perennial herb, longpod senna blooms once summer rains have started. It occurs from New Mexico and Arizona to South America.

Senna hirsuta (L.) Irwin & Barneby
   var. *glaberrima* (Jones) Irwin & Barneby
Pea Family

35·YELLOW SWEETCLOVER

Because roots of yellow sweetclover bind the soil, helping to prevent erosion where native vegetation has been destroyed, the Forest Service sometimes seeds yellow sweetclover after forest fires, and highway departments often sow it on roadside embankments. Like many roadside plants in the Southwest woodlands, yellow sweetclover is a European import. It has become naturalized in much of the United States, which means that it spreads from place to place without human intervention. Not a true clover, yellow sweetclover is more closely related to alfalfa (*Medicago sativa* L.). White sweetclover (*Melilotus albus* Desr.), also a common roadside weed, is another European introduction.

Melilotus officinalis (L.) Lam.
Pea Family

John Richardson

36·GREENE DEER VETCH

Charles T. Mason, Jr.

Greene deer vetch was named after Edward L. Greene, an Episcopal minister who was, by 1885, the leading botanist of the West and a rival to Asa Gray of Harvard. Greene is remembered today less for his botanical collections (though he did collect widely in the West) than for his uncompromising stand against Asa Gray, then the foremost American botanist. Unlike most other collectors in the western United States, who sent their specimens to Asa Gray so that he could describe any new species they might have discovered, Greene insisted on describing new species himself. While his independent stand was admirable, the result – hundreds of "new" species that have since been discredited – was simply confusing. Now that much of the confusion he planted has been weeded out, it seems appropriate that he be honored in Greene deer vetch, among other species. Greene deer vetch grows in woodlands in southern Arizona, southern New Mexico and northern Mexico. It blooms in spring and summer.

Lotus greenei (Woot. & Standl.) Ottley
Pea Family

37·YELLOW EVENING PRIMROSE

Take five minutes some summer evening to watch the flowers of yellow evening primrose open. Around sunset, the calyx tube, which tightly enfolds the furled petals, cracks along one side. The petals then start to unroll, pressing on the calyx. As the petals continue to unfold, the calyx slips down, until finally the four heart-shaped petals spring free of their confinement and fully expand. The fragrant flowers of yellow evening primrose attract hawkmoths in the evening, and, before they wilt the following morning, a few bees. A common plant in streambeds, yellow evening primrose is a biennial. The first year, it puts out only clusters of leaves. During the second year, the plants send up flowering stalks three or four feet tall. Yellow evening primrose grows from Kansas to Nevada and south to northern Mexico.

Oenothera hookeri Torr. & Gray
Evening Primrose Family

38·PUCCOON

Lithospermum, the genus name of puccoon, means stone seed, and indeed the seeds of puccoon are nearly rock-hard. The trumpet-shaped, yellow flowers that appear in spring and early summer are sometimes sterile – they produce no seeds. Later in the season, inconspicuous flowers that never fully open produce abundant seed. These inconspicuous flowers fertilize themselves in the bud without the assistance of insect visitors. The advantage of such self-pollination is that it assures seed production. Puccoon can still set seeds in years when pollinators are scarce or are more interested in other flowers. The disadvantage is that different puccoon plants are not mixing their genes to create new plants. Gene-mixing keeps plant populations variable and helps to ensure that at least a few individuals might survive should some environmental upheaval take place. Puccoon grows from western Texas to Arizona and Mexico.

Lithospermum cobrense Greene
Borage Family

George H.H. Huey

39·MULLEIN

Put a bit of mullein leaf on your blisters as you hike, one expert in medicinal plants has suggested – the soft, felty leaves will prevent further rubbing. Other uses of mullein in folk medicine include making a tea from the flowers for coughs and smoking the leaves for chest infections. A biennial, mullein puts out a rosette of furry, floppy leaves the first year and a tall flowering stalk the second. The plants are most abundant along roadsides and in other disturbed spots. A native of Europe, mullein has become well established throughout the temperate zone of North America. It flowers in the summer.

Verbascum thapsus L.
Figwort Family

40·BUTTER-
AND EGGS

A European import, butter-and-eggs is more plentiful than many native wildflowers along highways and in vacant lots. The tube of each bright yellow flower is prolonged into a nectar-containing spur. Only a strong insect such as a bumblebee can force the upper and lower lips of the flower apart to gain entrance to the blossom and thus reach the nectar in the spur. The orange spot on the lips is a nectar guide that shows bees how to approach the flower. Butter-and-eggs has naturalized throughout North America.

Linaria vulgaris Miller
Figwort Family

Larry Ulrich

41·SPOTTED MONKEYFLOWER

Spotted monkeyflower grows in streams, springs and seeps. The stems root at the nodes, forming clumps on cliffs and among streambed rocks. Flowers are bright yellow and spotted with red in one variety, unspotted in another. Self-pollination is prevented by movement of the stigmas. When a bee enters the flower in search of nectar, it brushes first against the two-lobed stigma, which then folds shut and lies pressed against the inside of the flower. The bee next contacts the anthers, takes nectar, and soon withdraws. No pollen from within the flower touches the closed stigmas as the bee leaves the blossom. The bee then carries pollen to the open stigmas of another flower. Spotted monkeyflower blooms from spring to fall and occurs throughout the West.

Mimulus guttatus DC.
Figwort Family

42·TRUMPET BUSH

Trumpet bush, a tropical plant, often grows on rocky slopes where boulders may afford it some protection from frost. Bumblebees pollinate the wide-mouthed yellow flowers by crawling all the way into the flower, then backing out. Carpenter bees are nectar thieves on trumpet bush flowers. Since these large, black bees are too big to squeeze all the way into the flower, they cut a hole near the base of the tube and illegitimately reach the nectar. Trumpet bush blooms in the summer and grows from southern Arizona and New Mexico into tropical America.

Tecoma stans (L.) H.B.K.
Bignonia Family

43·BUFFALO GOURD

Every summer, the long trailing stems of buffalo gourd smother roadside embankments and clamber over barbed-wire fences. The lushness of the vine is not surprising given the tremendous size of its root. One buffalo gourd taproot weighed in at 159 pounds. The large leaves smell like dirty socks – thus the species name *foetidissima,* which means fetid. A wild relative of cultivated squashes and melons, buffalo gourd bears fruits the size of tennis balls at the end of the summer. These are as distasteful as the leaves are malodorous, and if you are incautious enough to taste the flesh, its bitterness will linger in your mouth for hours. Buffalo gourd flowers, like those of most squashes, open quite early in the day, sometimes before dawn. Even so, the squash and gourd bees, which depend exclusively on wild gourd flowers for pollen and nectar, are up in time to pollinate the flowers. Sometimes you can find these bees asleep in the closed flowers later in the day. Buffalo gourd grows from Missouri and Nebraska to Texas, Arizona, southern California and Mexico.

Cucurbita foetidissima H.B.K.
Squash Family

44·TELEGRAPH PLANT

Telegraph plant is one of about 20,000 species in the Sunflower Family, the largest plant family in the world. A single sunflower blossom is actually a multitude of flowers. Each of the ray "petals" is a separate flower, as is each of the tiny tubes in the central disk. Every flower sits atop an ovule, and if fertilized, every ovule develops into a one-seeded fruit called an achene. Although telegraph plant is native to the United States, it acts like a weed, and thrives in such disturbed places as old fields, roadsides, vacant lots and pastures. Like many native weeds, telegraph plant has a wide elevational range and grows from the desert into the mountains. When crushed, the leaves give off a pungent odor of camphor, thus the alternate common name of camphorweed. Telegraph plant blooms in the summer and occurs throughout the United States.

Heterotheca subaxillaris (Lam.) Britt. & Rusby
Sunflower Family

45·SNAKEWEED

A plant as common and obnoxious as snakeweed is bound to have multiple common names, and snakeweed is also known as matchweed, snakebroom, broomweed, turpentineweed and resinweed. Most of these names reflect the low esteem in which snakeweed is held, expecially by ranchers. Because cattle won't eat snakeweed, the plants multiply rapidly on rangeland. (Where abundant, snakeweed indicates an overgrazed range.) Hispanic and Native Americans found beneficial uses for snakeweed, however; they made tea from the leaves and stems for rheumatism, malaria and snakebite. Snakeweed blooms in the late summer and fall and occurs throughout the West.

Gutierrezia sarothrae (Pursh) Britt. & Rusby
Sunflower Family

46·TURPENTINEBUSH

The flowering of turpentinebush signals the end of summer and the arrival of fall in desert grassland and oak woodland. Small, golden-yellow flower heads cover the shrubs, attracting a variety of bees, beetles and other insects. By blooming late in the year, turpentinebush avoids competition with summer wildflowers for pollinators and ensures that insects will eagerly seek out the nectar and pollen it has to offer. Turpentinebush might be confused with snakeweed, but the two can be distinguished readily: leaves of turpentinebush are clustered toward the stem tip, whereas those of snakeweed are evenly distributed along the entire stem. Also, turpentinebush leaves are short and leathery, those of snakeweed long and flexible. Turpentinebush grows on rocky slopes from western Texas to Arizona and northern Mexico.

Ericameria laricifolia (Gray) Shinners
Sunflower Family

George H.H. Huey

47·RUBBER RABBITBRUSH

Just as the blooming of turpentinebush signals the arrival of fall in the oak woodlands, so the flowering of rubber rabbitbrush announces the arrival of autumn in pinyon-juniper country. The paucity of other wildflowers at that time of year makes rubber rabbitbrush more attractive to insects. By being the only game in town, rubber rabbitbrush avoids the frenzied midsummer competition for pollinators. Navajo Indians cut the flowering branches and use the twigs and blossoms to make dyes of various shades of yellow. Rubber rabbitbrush thrives along roads, in valley bottoms and on disturbed sites. One variety or another occurs from Saskatchewan to British Columbia and south to west Texas, southern California and northern Mexico.

Chrysothamnus nauseosus (Pall.) Britt.
Sunflower Family

48·SPARSE-FLOWERED GOLDENROD

Goldenrods are a familiar sight in pastures, bottomlands and roadsides throughout the United States. The single-sided arrangement of flower heads on their branches is characteristic of sparse-flowered goldenrod, among others. Each flower head contains about a dozen disk and ray flowers. The tiny tubes of the disk flowers hold miniscule amounts of nectar – less than one microliter each. (In comparison, the hummingbird-pollinated flowers of skyrocket secrete six to eight microliters of nectar each day, and the bat-pollinated flowers of Palmer agave produce about 700 microliters every night.) The insignificant nectar production of individual goldenrod flowers is somewhat compensated by the large number of flowers on a single plant. Even the sparse-flowered goldenrod produces many times more flowers per plant than either skyrocket or Palmer agave. Sparse-flowered goldenrod flowers in summer and fall.

Solidago sparsiflora Gray
Sunflower Family

49·PRAIRIE ZINNIA

At first glance, prairie zinnia doesn't look much like a member of the Sunflower Family. Still, each ray *is* a separate flower, as are each of the approximately two dozen tubular flowers in the center of the head. The rays turn papery with age and remain attached to the achenes. When the achenes of the ray flowers finally fall from the heads, the rays become wings that blow in the wind, thus dispersing the seeds. Disk achenes, lacking any wings, fall near the parent plant. Prairie zinnia hedges its bets: some seeds stay in a place that has already proved suitable while others take a chance on colonizing new areas. Most wild zinnias grow in the subtropics, but prairie zinnia can be found from Kansas to Nevada and south to northern Mexico. It flowers in the summer.

Zinnia grandiflora Nutt.
Sunflower Family

50·BLANKETFLOWER

Blanketflower is readily recognized by the maroon to purple centers and deeply toothed, yellow rays. Insects undoubtedly notice the contrast between the ray and disk flowers: the combination of yellow and purple is particularly attractive to bees. (Bees also like yellow with blue, orange with blue, yellow with violet and white with various colors.) It seems likely that the contrasting colors of a blanketflower direct insects to the pollen and nectar in the disk flowers and perhaps even help insects distinguish blanketflower from other wildflowers. Blanketflower grows on plains and along roadsides from Colorado and Utah to Texas, Arizona and New Mexico and blooms from spring to fall.

Gaillardia pinnatifida Torr.
Sunflower Family

51·MANY-FLOWERED GOLDENEYE

Many-flowered goldeneye, a perennial herb of roadsides and rocky slopes, usually blooms in late summer and fall. Goldeneyes are closely related to the common sunflower but have yellow rather than brown centers. Though we call them goldeneyes because of their yellow centers, the flower heads aren't goldeneyed at all, as far as bees are concerned. Bees can see colors that humans cannot – ultraviolet, for example – and so perceive patterns in flowers that we miss entirely. The yellow center of many-flowered goldeneye is colored by ultraviolet, making a strong contrast (as far as bees are concerned) with the yellow-tipped rays. It's hard for us to imagine exactly what many-flowered goldeneye looks like to a bee; perhaps the flower heads of blanketflower are as close as we can get. Many-flowered goldeneye occurs from southwestern Montana to New Mexico, southern Arizona, Nevada and eastern California.

Viguiera multiflora (Nutt.) Blake
Sunflower Family

52·NAVAJO TEA

A perennial herb, Navajo tea grows along roadsides and in woodland openings from Nebraska and Wyoming to Texas, Arizona and Mexico. Navajo Indians use the leaves, stems and flowers to dye wool: dried plants combined with alum make an orange dye; fresh plants with no additives make light olive green. Navajo tea is a traditional medicinal herb among Hispanic New Mexicans, who call it *cota*. Tea made from the dried stems and leaves reportedly has a pleasantly piney, sweet flavor and can be used as a mild diuretic. Navajo tea blooms throughout the summer.

Thelesperma megapotamicum (Spreng.)
Kuntze
Sunflower Family

53·THREADLEAF GROUNDSEL

All parts of threadleaf groundsel are toxic to livestock and humans. Cattle usually avoid the plants when there is anything else to eat, but people have been known to confuse the felty, gray leaves with those of *gordolobo (Gnaphalium* sp.), a beneficial herb, with fatal results. A shrub to four feet tall, threadleaf groundsel blooms sporadically throughout the year. It is closely related to the desert groundsel *(Senecio douglasii* DC. var. *douglasii)*, an annual wildflower of low elevations. Threadleaf groundsel grows on plains and in washes from Colorado and Utah to Texas and Mexico.

Senecio douglasii DC.
    var. *longilobus* (Benth.) L. Benson
Sunflower Family

54·NEW MEXICO GROUNDSEL

A variety of bees, flies, beetles and butterflies visit the yellow blossoms of New Mexico groundsel. Yellow has general appeal in the insect world, and most yellow-flowered plants can count on receiving a wide array of insect visitors, although some of them, such as flies, may not be very efficient pollinators, and others, such as beetles, may actually do more harm than good by eating pollen or petals. A common perennial herb of woodlands and pine forests, New Mexico groundsel blooms in the spring and summer. It is one of the most abundant and widespread species of *Senecio* in Southwest woodlands and can be found in Colorado, New Mexico and Arizona.

Senecio neomexicanus Gray
Sunflower Family

55·FLAME FLOWER

The species name of flame flower, *aurantiacum*, means orange and comes from the coppery petals. Flame Flower is a perennial herb that sprouts from thick, woody roots and produces flowers once summer rains have begun. Like many plants in the Portulaca Family, flame flower has succulent leaves. Flame flower can be common on grassy slopes or in openings among oaks from west Texas to southern Arizona and northern Mexico.

Talinum aurantiacum Engelm.
Portulaca Family

56·BUTTERFLYWEED

Butterflyweed is notable among the milkweeds for its vermillion to yellow flowers and for the absence of milky sap in the stems and leaves. Many small flowers join together to create the broad, flat-topped clusters typical of butterflyweed. Presumably, the broader and brighter the cluster, the more insects it will attract. There are limits to this strategy, however. Once a flower cluster becomes too large, insects spend all their time on one cluster, and instead of carrying pollen from plant to plant, they take it only from flower to flower. Since butterflyweed flowers cannot set fruit with pollen from the same plant, fruit production is poor on clusters that are too broad. Butterflyweed grows throughout the United States.

Asclepias tuberosa L.
Milkweed Family

John Richardson

57·INDIAN PINK

The five, jagged, red petals of Indian pink make it instantly recognizable. A perennial herb pollinated mainly by hummingbirds, Indian pink blooms in the summer on shaded slopes, often with oaks and pines, from west Texas to California and Mexico. Hummingbird-pollinated flowers have evolved in one plant family after another. Most share certain characteristics: red color; long, narrow tubes; spreading or turned-back petals; and abundant nectar. Indian pink certainly fits the bill, even though it belongs to a family in which the petals are separate rather than fused into tubes. How can this be? If you look closely at an Indian pink flower, you'll see that the lower part of each petal is confined within a tubular calyx, like stems of garden flowers confined within a vase. Thus Indian pink has kept the separate petals typical of the Pink Family while displaying the tubular shape so attractive to hummingbirds.

Silene laciniata Cav.
Pink Family

58·CORAL BELLS

Coral bells gets its alternate common name of alum root from the astringent properties of the dried root, which is rich in tannin. Tea made from the roots is a folk remedy for dysentery and reportedly also makes an excellent gargle for sore throats.

The plants most often grow in the shade of boulders and cliffs in Arizona and northern Mexico. Coral bells blooms in spring and summer.

Heuchera sanguinea Engelm.
Saxifrage Family

Charles T. Mason, Jr.

59·CORAL BEAN

Whether in flower or in fruit, coral bean is one of the most striking plants in the Southwest. Much of the year, however, the leafless brown stems are scarcely noticeable in their rocky hillside habitat. In June, clusters of red flowers sprout from the stem tips, attracting hummingbirds which probe the tubular blossoms for nectar. Three-parted leaves appear once the summer rains are underway, usually in July. Coral bean plants are most conspicuous in the autumn when their leaves have turned golden and the brown pods gape open revealing vermillion (occasionally tan) seeds. Alkaloids make coral bean seeds highly toxic. In the Southwest, winter temperatures prevent coral bean from growing much taller than three feet, but in the frost-free parts of northern Mexico, it is a small tree up to twenty feet tall. Coral bean occurs in Arizona, New Mexico and northern Mexico.

Erythrina flabelliformis Kearney
Pea Family

60·CLARET CUPS HEDGEHOG

We don't generally think of cacti as mountain plants, but claret cups hedgehog weathers the winters up to 9000 feet above sea level. Another unusual thing about this cactus is that it is pollinated by hummingbirds instead of bees. Attracting hummingbird pollinators involved evolutionary modifications of the usual cactus blueprint. Instead of the dish-shaped flowers typical of the hedgehog group, claret cups has trumpet-shaped flowers. And instead of flowers in various shades of pink and purple, claret cups hedgehog has bright red ones. Several varieties of claret cups hedgehog grow in the Southwest, usually on boulder outcrops, in southeastern California, southern Nevada, Colorado, Arizona, New Mexico, west Texas and south to central Mexico. It blooms in the spring.

Larry Ulrich

Echinocereus triglochidiatus Engelm.
Cactus Family

61·HUMMINGBIRD TRUMPET

Like most of the red, tubular flowers in the Southwest, hummingbird trumpet is pollinated largely by hummingbirds. As a hummingbird probes the flower for nectar, the protruding stamens brush pollen on the bird's head. A plant of streamsides and shaded banks, hummingbird trumpet blooms sporadically from spring to fall.

The slender pods split open to reveal many small seeds, each tufted with white hairs that float them through the air. Hummingbird trumpet occurs from New Mexico to Arizona, Oregon, California and Sonora.

Epilobium canum (Greene) Raven
Evening Primrose Family

62·SCARLET CREEPER

The bright red flowers of scarlet creeper hardly resemble the familiar morning glories of gardens and fields. In the Morning Glory Family, as in many other plant families, certain species have evolved to attract hummingbirds as pollinators. Hummingbird flowers share particular characteristics: red color; long, narrow tubes; spreading or turned-back petals;

and abundant nectar. Scarlet creeper, though uncharacteristic of morning glories as a group, certainly is typical of hummingbird flowers. A vine of roadsides and woodland clearings, scarlet creeper occurs from western Texas to Arizona and south into tropical America.

Ipomoea coccinea L.
Morning Glory Family

63·SKYROCKET

A single flower of skyrocket contains little nectar by human standards. Left undisturbed for twenty-four hours, a flower will accumulate just six to eight microliters of nectar, less than a teardrop's worth of fluid. But where many skyrockets grow together, a hummingbird can find an ample supply of nectar. Skyrocket has evolved with hummingbirds over thousands of years so that each is perfectly suited to the other. The floral tubes of skyrocket just fit the bills of the hummingbirds. The red is quickly recognized by birds, and since few insects can see red, the nectar in the flowers is essentially reserved for hummingbirds. Also, the lobes of each flower are bent backwards. This permits hummingbirds free access to the flowers but prevents bees from landing. Despite these precautions, certain bees learn to rob skyrocket flowers of nectar by slitting the flower tubes at the base and extracting nectar. Skyrocket blooms throughout the summer along roadsides and in woodland clearings over much of the West.

Ipomopsis aggregata (Pursh) V. Grant
Phlox Family

64·BETONY

Betony is one of many red-flowered plants that provide a reliable nectar source late in the summer for hummingbirds as they migrate through the Southwest into Mexico and Central America. Betony often blooms at the same time as Indian paintbrush, bouvardia, scarlet penstemon and Indian pink, all plants with the tubular, red flowers that attract hummingbirds. The paired leaves and square stems typical of the Mint Family, combined with the two-lipped vermillion flowers, make betony easy to recognize. The plants thrive on shaded banks and under trees from western Texas to southern Arizona and Mexico. Betony blooms in spring and summer.

Stachys coccinea Jacq.
Mint Family

John Richardson

65·INDIAN PAINTBRUSH

Even expert botanists have difficulty differentiating among the two hundred species of Indian paintbrush in western North America. Indian paintbrush flowers are inconspicuous: it is the bright red bracts beneath each flower that catch the eye. Most, if not all, species of Indian paintbrush are hemiparasitic and depend on host plants to supply water and nutrients. Indian paintbrush seedlings grow poorly or won't grow at all if the plants fail to find a host. Like most hemiparasites, even fully grown plants of Indian paintbrush lack a well-developed root system. The underground portion of the plant consists of special conducting tubes, called haustoria, that attach to the roots of the host (often oaks or grasses in the Southwest). The Figwort Family contains many hemiparasites, including owl's clover (*Orthocarpus purpurascens* Benth.), a desert wildflower.

Castilleja linariaefolia Benth.
Figwort Family

Scarlet penstemon is one of about fifty hummingbird flowers in the Southwest and one of forty species of penstemon in western North America that are pollinated by hummingbirds. The flowers are tailor-made for hummingbird pollination. Since birds can see red but bees cannot, the red flowers appeal to hummingbirds and are usually overlooked by bees. Since the flowers are tubular, with the lower lip bent back, a hummingbird can hover to sip nectar, but butterflies and bees, which must perch in order to feed, can find no convenient foothold. Although scarlet penstemon superficially resembles skyrocket, it's easy to tell them apart. Leaves of scarlet penstemon arise in pairs on the stem and have smooth margins, whereas those of skyrocket arise singly and are cut into many narrow segments. Also, flowers of scarlet penstemon are distinctly two-lipped, those of skyrocket divided into five identical lobes. Scarlet penstemon blooms throughout the summer and occurs from southern Colorado and Utah to central Mexico.

Penstemon barbatus (Cav.) Roth
Figwort Family

66·SCARLET PENSTEMON

67·BOUVARDIA

Stephen Trimble

Another of the many hummingbird flowers in southwestern woodlands, bouvardia blooms on shaded slopes once summer rains are well underway. Although the tubular, red flowers are designed to attract hummingbirds, butterflies also occasionally visit the flowers. (Even though most insects can't see red, a few species of butterflies can.) The nectar of typical hummingbird flowers differs from that of typical butterfly flowers in several ways. One of the most important is that hummingbirds require large amounts of dilute nectar, whereas insects thrive on small quantities of sticky, viscous nectar. The distinction is not absolute, however. Desert hummingbirds visit such typical bee flowers as creosote bush [*Larrea tridentata* (DC.) Cov.] and blue paloverde (*Cercidium floridum* Benth.) when hummingbird flowers are scarce, just as certain butterflies work bouvardia and other characteristic hummingbird blossoms. Bouvardia belongs to a largely tropical family and occurs from Arizona and New Mexico to northern Mexico.

Bouvardia ternifolia (Cav.) Schlecht.
Madder Family

68·ARIZONA THISTLE

In the summertime, hummingbirds, butterflies and bumblebees all visit the bright red flower heads of the Arizona thistle, a common plant along roadsides in Arizona. As in all members of the Sunflower Family, each head of Arizona Thistle actually contains many flowers. An individual thistle flower is a narrow tube with five long, red lobes, each tipped with yellow. When clustered by the hundreds into a single flower head, the yellow tips resemble pollen and probably attract bees to the flowers. (Bees can't see red, but they home right in on yellow.) Since most thistles in the Southwest have broad heads that point straight up, it seems likely that the narrow, tilted heads of Arizona thistle evolved as a way of appealing to hummingbirds, which have learned to associate red, tubular, tilted flowers with nectar.

Cirsium arizonicum (Gray) Petrak
Sunflower Family

Stewart Aitchison

Larry Ulrich

69·WILD FOUR O'CLOCK

Flowers of wild four o'clock open late in the day, usually after sundown, and close as the following day begins. Scentless by day, the flowers start to emit a musky fragrance about two hours after they open, and within ten minutes the odor begins to attract hawkmoths. These large-bodied moths are the major pollinators of wild four o'clock flowers. Although bees sometimes gather pollen from the blossoms early in the morning, they effect little pollination. Wild four o'clock thrives on rocky slopes and along roadsides. It blooms throughout the summer and can be found from Colorado and Utah to northern Mexico.

Mirabilis multiflora (Torr.) Gray
Four O'Clock Family

70·ROCKY MOUNTAIN BEEPLANT

Larry Ulrich

Rocky mountain beeplant colors fields and roadsides pink when it blooms in the summer. The delicate flowers are much visited by bees; in fact, beekeepers sometimes cultivate Rocky Mountain beeplant as a ready source of nectar. The Navajo, who occasionally use the tender young plants as greens, hold Rocky Mountain beeplant in high regard because it has saved the tribe from starvation more than once. Rocky Mountain beeplant occurs from Saskatchewan south to Arizona, east to Kansas and west to Oregon.

Cleome serrulata Pursh
Caper Family

71·WILD ROSE

The wild rose is no less beautiful than its domesticated relative. Pollination of the dish-shaped flowers happens by what one botanist has called "mess and soil:" in messing about on the blossoms, insects inadvertently transfer pollen from the anthers of one plant to the stigmas of another. The Rose Family is particularly important in the northern part of the Southwest where woodlands of pinyon and juniper replace those of oak and pine. In pinyon-juniper country, a panoply of Rose Family members, among them fern bush, cliff rose, Apache plume and Utah serviceberry, occupies canyon slopes and mesa tops. In part, this abundance of roses and their relatives occurs because the Rose Family has temperate affinities, and is well suited to the cold, snowy winters and mild summers of the pinyon-juniper region. One species or another of wild rose occurs throughout temperate North America. The most common species in the West, *Rosa woodsii,* can be found from Saskatchewan to British Columbia and south to Arizona, New Mexico and Texas.

George H.H. Huey

Rosa woodsii Lindl.
Rose Family

72·GATUÑO

Pretty enough to be grown in gardens, gatuño can be abundant on rocky slopes and along roadsides in desert grassland and oak woodland. Each pink spike is composed of numerous flowers that fade from pink to white as they age. The petals themselves are hardly noticeable; rather, it is the pink filaments of the numerous stamens that catch your eye. Gatuño belongs to the Pea Family and, within that family, to the Mimosa Subfamily. The many species of mesquite and acacia also belong to the Mimosoideae, an important subfamily in the tropics and subtropics. Gatuño, a summer-flowering shrub, grows from western Texas to southern Arizona and northern Mexico.

Mimosa dysocarpa Benth.
Pea Family

73·WILD BEAN

Vines of wild bean clamber on banks and slopes after summer rains have started. Each part of the highly stylized bean flower has its own name and function. The single upright petal – called the banner – serves to attract the attention of pollinators, typically solitary bees. The two side petals – the wings – serve as a landing platform for the bee. The coiled petals – called the keel – between the wings hold the style and stamens. When a bee lands on the wings, its weight depresses them, causing the stamens and style to shoot out from the keel and dust the bee with pollen on its underside. Wild bean blooms in the summer and bears small, beanlike pods in the fall. It occurs in southern Arizona and Mexico.

Phaseolus ritensis Jones
Pea Family

74·FEATHER PLUME

A miniature, intricately branched shrub, feather plume thrives on rocky slopes from Arizona to Oklahoma and northern Mexico. In the Southwest, it most frequently grows on limestone. The flowers, with their cream-colored banner petals and magenta wings, are small but colorful. Bees are probably the most important pollinators of feather plume. Small butterflies that sip the nectar by inserting their tongues between the banner and keel are nectar thieves, since they remove nectar without pollinating the blossoms in return.

Dalea formosa Torr.
Pea Family

75·NEW MEXICO LOCUST

After a forest fire, New Mexico locust is often one of the first woody plants to become abundant on the burned site. Because the roots sprout readily, New Mexico Locust quickly forms thickets, thus holding the soil in place and helping to prevent the erosion that would otherwise occur after fire. Like many Pea Family members, New Mexico locust adds nitrogen to the soil, and wildflowers underneath the plants often grow more luxuriantly than those a short distance away. In the late spring and early summer, large clusters of pink to lavender flowers attract bumblebees and hummingbirds. New Mexico locust grows with oaks and pines from southern Colorado and southern Nevada to west Texas, New Mexico, Arizona and northern Mexico.

Robinia neomexicana Gray
Pea Family

76·LAMBERT LOCOWEED

Livestock, like people, can become addicted to substances that are not good for them, Lambert locoweed for one. Though the plants are dangerous to cattle, sheep and horses, causing listlessness, staggers, blindness and eventually death, some animals will eat locoweeds when grass is scarce and may even develop an addiction to the plants. Ironically, Lambert locoweed is apt to be most abundant – and therefore most readily available – on overgrazed ranges. The silvery foliage and magenta to purple flowers are very attractive. Lambert locoweed occurs throughout the West.

Oxytropis lambertii Pursh
Pea Family

77·BUSHY TICK CLOVER

The tick clovers are named for the ticklike way the stems and pods cling to clothing. Their adhesive quality comes from numerous small hairs tipped with microscopic barbs. Tick clover pods don't split into halves like most legumes; instead, they break into one-seeded segments that fasten onto animals or people. In this way, the seeds are dispersed. Bushy tick clover is a sprawling perennial often found under oaks and along washes. It flowers throughout the summer and occurs from southern New Mexico and Arizona to northern Mexico.

Desmodium batocaulon Gray
Pea Family

78·CRANE'S BILL

The crane's bill, or wild geranium, grows profusely on roadside embankments or singly along shaded trails. Its lavender to pink flowers attract small bees which forage for nectar at the base of the central column made by the five styles and ten stamens. The stamens are curved backwards into an arcade, and as the bee circles under them, her back brushes against the anthers and collects pollen. When she visits the next flower, pollen rubs off onto the curved styles. The five small knobs at the base of the central column are ovaries, that is, immature seed pods. As the ovaries ripen, they snap loose and curl upwards, flinging the seeds into the air. Crane's bill can be found from Colorado and Utah to western Texas, Arizona, New Mexico and Mexico.

Geranium caespitosum James
Geranium Family

79·JATROPHA

Some wild plants with large, starchy roots make fine eating, but the enlarged root of jatropha is strongly purgative and should be considered poisonous. Jatropha is monoecious, which means literally "one household." In practice, it means that stamens and pistils are found in separate flowers on the same plant. (Dioecious plants – those with two households – feature male or female flowers on separate plants.) The three-lobed fruits of jatropha are characteristic of the Spurge Family. When the capsules are ripe, they open explosively, flinging the seeds some distance from the parent plant. Jatropha can be abundant on grassy slopes and openings in oak woodland from southern Arizona and New Mexico into Mexico.

Jatropha macrorhiza Benth.
Spurge Family

80·FENDLER GLOBE MALLOW

Fendler globe mallow is one of about twenty species of globe mallow in the Southwest. The brushlike column of stamens in the center of the flower is characteristic of the Mallow Family. Bumblebees collect pollen from the pink flowers by straddling the column and brushing the pollen from the anthers onto their fuzzy abdomens. Small solitary bees in the genus *Diadasia* are also important pollinators of this and other globe mallows. Occasionally abundant on disturbed sites and at roadsides among oaks and pines, Fendler globe mallow can be found from southern Colorado to western Texas and Arizona. It blooms in the summer.

Sphaeralcea fendleri Gray
Mallow Family

81·PORCUPINE PRICKLY PEAR

The species name of this prickly pear, *erinacea*, means hedgehog and refers to its long, downward-pointing spines. Flower color varies from rose to deep pink to yellow, depending on the variety. Of the many insect visitors to the flowers, bees are the most important pollinators. In approaching the flowers, a bee lands on the stigma, then crawls into the stamens, ermerging some time later liberally dusted with pollen which it carries to the stigma of the next flower. Touch the stamens of a prickly pear flower and watch them curl and twist inward. This movement is thought to be a mechanism for dumping more pollen on the bees, thus making pollination more efficient. The five varieties of this prickly pear can be found from southeastern Washington and Idaho to southeastern California and central New Mexico. Porcupine prickly pear flowers in May and June.

Opuntia erinacea Engelm. & Bigel.
Cactus Family

John Richardson

82·CANE CHOLLA

The chollas and prickly pears are easy to tell apart – cholla joints are cylindrical; prickly pear pads are flat. Both joints and pads are modified stems that store water against drought. The fleshy stems of cane cholla are supported by hollow, netted cylinders of wood that last long after the pulpy tissue has decayed. Sometimes curio stores sell canes and other novelties made from cholla wood, thus the common name cane cholla. Flowers of cane cholla are small compared to many other cactus flowers and vary in color from plant to plant – purple, red, yellow or, rarely, white. Cane cholla can attain heights of six feet or more. It grows from Arizona and New Mexico to Sonora and Chihuahua.

Opuntia spinosior (Engelm.) Toumey
Cactus Family

Charles T. Mason, Jr.

83·RAINBOW CACTUS

Bands of alternating pink and white spines give rainbow cactus its common name. The species name *pectinatus* means toothed, like a comb, and refers to the comblike clusters of the spines. The purplish lavender flowers sometimes seem too large for the squat stems. Rainbow cactus grows on rocky slopes in desert grassland and oak woodland. Several varieties occur from Arizona to Texas and south into Mexico.

Echinocereus pectinatus (Scheidw.) Engelm.
Cactus Family

George H.H. Huey

84·HEN-AND-CHICKS

If you look carefully at the stem of hen-and-chicks, you'll see that it is made of many small nipplelike protrusions. These are called tubercules. Flowers always arise on the newly developing tubercles of the season. In fact, *Coryphantha,* the genus name of hen-and-chicks, means "top flower," referring to the position of the flowers on the stem. Often a single plant will form mounds composed of multiple stems – up to 200 in one variety – leading to the common name hen-and-chicks. Translated literally, the species name *vivipara* means bearing the young alive, which also refers to the multiple stems. Several varieties of hen-and-chicks occur throughout the Southwest. Not all produce multiple stems.

Coryphantha vivipara (Nutt.) Britton & Rose
Cactus Family

Charles T. Mason, Jr.

85·PINK-THROATED MORNING GLORY

Most of us have seen small ants at sugar bowls or hummingbird feeders. These ants eat sugar in the wild, too. One possible source is the nectaries inside flowers, but unfortunately for the ants, access to nectaries is usually difficult. Many plants provide nectaries outside the flowers as well, on leaves, stems or sepals. Pink-throated morning glory supplies nectar to ants in nectaries on its sepals. In return, the ants act as policemen, keeping plant-sucking bugs from damaging the plants. Stems of pink-throated morning glory trail across the ground flourishing trumpet-shaped flowers suffused with red-violet inside. It occurs from Oklahoma to southern Arizona and Mexico and blooms in the summer.

Ipomoea longifolia Benth.
Morning Glory Family

86·DAKOTA VERBENA

Dakota verbena is typical of butterfly-pollinated wildflowers. The blossoms are hot pink, a favorite color of butterflies, and the flat-topped flower clusters make convenient landing platforms. Sometimes other long-tongued insects — hover flies, for instance — visit verbena flowers, but most bees don't have tongues long enough to reach the nectar. Certain bees, however, have evolved special bristles on their front legs that enable them to collect pollen by inserting their forelegs into the tube. Dakota verbena grows in woodland openings and can be abundant on burned sites. It occurs from Alabama to Arizona, north to South Dakota, and far south into Mexico.

Glandularia bipinnatifida (Nutt.) Nutt.
Verbena Family

87·SHOWY PENSTEMON

The genus name *Penstemon* means five stamens. If you look inside a flower, however, you'll see only four stamens. The fifth stamen, called a staminode, has lost its anther. Since most species in the Figwort Family truly do possess only four stamens it seems likely that the fifth stamen – the staminode – in *Penstemon* must serve some purpose. One possibility is that, by blocking the narrow tube at the bottom of the flower, the staminode prevents tiny insects from penetrating deeply enough into the blossom to steal nectar. Showy penstemon commonly occurs under trees in oak woodland. Its leaves will help you distinguish it from other southwestern penstemons: they are sharply toothed and encircle the stem. Occasionally showy penstemon creeps down from the oak woodland into the desert, where it can be found on shaded slopes and in washes. A spring-blooming perennial, showy penstemon occurs from southwestern New Mexico to eastern California.

George H.H. Huey

Penstemon pseudospectabilis Jones
Figwort Family

88·PALMER PENSTEMON

The lightbulb-shaped flowers of Palmer penstemon evolved to accommodate large-bodied bees such as the black carpenter bees and the black and yellow bumblebees. As a bee enters the ample flowers, anthers dust its back with pollen. When the bee goes to another flower of Palmer penstemon, the drooping stigma picks up some of the pollen grains. Purple lines on the inside of the pale pink flowers guide bees to nectar in the short tube. A spring-blooming perennial, Palmer penstemon grows along roadsides and in washes in Utah, Arizona and California.

Penstemon palmeri Gray
Figwort Family

George H.H. Huey

89·THURBER PEREZIA

A perennial herb, Thurber perezia is easily recognized by the tall, leafy stems topped with wide clusters of pinkish-lavender blossoms. The honey-scented flowers attract many bees and butterflies. Individual flowers are two-lipped: one lip looks like a small ray and has three teeth, the other is simply a pair of lobes. Thurber perezia occurs on rocky slopes from southern Arizona and southern New Mexico to central Mexico. A similar species – brownfoot [*Acourtia wrightii* (Gray) Reveal & King] – is more widely distributed in the Southwest, occurring from west Texas to southern Utah, Arizona and northern Mexico. Brownfoot has eight to eleven flowers in each head, Thurber perezia only four to six.

Acourtia thurberi (Gray) Reveal & King
Sunflower Family

90·UNICORN PLANT

When the sickle-shaped pod of the unicorn plant splits open, the long beak becomes two claws that hook onto the leg of any passing animal, thus dispersing the seeds inside the pod. These hooks give unicorn plant its alternate common name of devil's claw. The fibers of the pod have been a traditional source of basket-making materials for Tohono O'odham (Papago) and Pima Indians. Long ago, the Indians domesticated a race of unicorn plant by selecting those plants with the longest claws and breeding them until the claws of the domesticated variety were twice as long as those growing wild. (The longer the pods, the better-suited their fibers for basketry.) The Indians still grow the unicorn plant in their gardens and harvest its fibers for basket-making. The wild variety thrives along roadsides and in other disturbed spots from western Texas to southern Nevada, Arizona, southern California and northern Mexico. Unicorn plant flowers in the summer.

Proboscidea parviflora (Woot.) Woot. & Standl.
Unicorn Plant Family

91·PRAIRIE SPIDERWORT

The common spiderwort in the eastern United States, *Tradescantia virginiana,* was introduced into England during the time of Charles the First, and it was soon developed into a common garden flower. In fact, the genus is named after John Tradescant, who was head gardener to Charles the First. You may already be familiar with the genus *Tradescantia* – several of the trailing species are grown as house plants under the name Wandering Jew. In the Southwest, *Tradescantia* is neither a garden flower nor a house plant but a small, succulent herb found in shallow soil on bedrock outcrops. Notice the six stamens in the center of each three-petaled flower: the filaments are plumed like a feather with fine, crinkly hairs. Prairie spiderwort occurs from Wisconsin to Montana, Texas and Arizona.

Tradescantia occidentalis (Britton) Smyth
Spiderwort Family

92·MANY-FLOWERED GILIA

Small as the lavender blossoms of many-flowered gilia are, each is large enough to convey a message in the form of purple speckles on the lower lip. These marks serve as a guide to show bees the way to nectar inside the flower tubes. Many-flowered gilia is one of several gilias common in southwestern woodlands. Different species of gilia attract different pollinators. The bluish to lavender flowers and short tubes of many-flowered gilia work especially well to attract bees. The pale lavender flowers and long tubes of Thurber gilia are adapted to pollination by night-flying moths. The medium-length tubes and bright red flowers of skyrocket appeal particularly to hummingbirds. Many-flowered gilia blooms in summer in Nevada, Arizona and New Mexico.

Ipomopsis multiflora (Nutt.) V. Grant
Phlox Family

93·THURBER GILIA

One of the prettiest wildflowers in the Southwest, Thurber gilia features drooping, lavender flowers clustered on one side of the stem. The long tubes and turned-back petals make the flowers inaccessible to bees and butterflies, which need to perch while feeding. Hawkmoths, which hover as they feed, are the main pollinators of Thurber gilia. What keeps hummingbirds from visiting the flowers for nectar? Since the flowers are not red, they are not as likely to catch a hummingbird's attention. Also, the tubes are probably too long for the hummingbirds that pass through our area: most of their bills measure one-third to three-quarters of an inch long, about half the length of a Thurber gilia flower. Thurber gilia can be abundant along roadsides after summer rains in Arizona, New Mexico and northern Mexico.

Ipomopsis thurberi (Torr.) V. Grant
Phlox Family

94·HYSSOP PENNYROYAL

Big bumblebees look comical at the tiny flowers of hyssop pennyroyal, but oddly enough, the little, lavender blossoms are quite well suited to bumblebee pollination. The lobes on the lower lip of the blossom provide a foothold for the bee, which must perch while it feeds. Anthers pressed against the ceiling of the blossom dust pollen on top of the bee as it pushes into the flower to get the nectar in the tube. *Hyssopifolium,* the species name of hyssop pennyroyal, means hyssop-leaved and refers to the stiff, crowded, narrow leaves. When crushed, the foliage smells like spearmint due to the release of volatile oils. Hyssop pennyroyal blooms from spring to fall along trails and on slopes in woodland and forest from New Mexico and Arizona to northern Mexico.

Hedeoma hyssopifolium Gray
Mint Family

95·DAYFLOWER

The structure of a dayflower is more complex than it appears at first glance. Of the six stamens, only the lower three are fertile. Two of these contain white pollen that the bee unknowingly carries from flower to flower: these are the fertilizing anthers. The central, or feeding, anther contains bright yellow pollen which the bee intentionally collects for its own use. Although an attractive shade of yellow, the upper stamens are devoid of pollen and never split open like normal anthers. These false anthers probably help make the flowers more attractive to bees and other insects. Dayflower blooms in the summer and can be found in woodland openings from New Mexico and Arizona far south into Mexico.

Commelina dianthifolia Delile
Spiderwort Family

96·ROCKY MOUNTAIN IRIS

Almost everyone knows the garden iris. Rocky Mountain iris is a scaled-down but no less beautiful version of the same basic flower. The three central "petals" are actually modified styles, as you can see by pulling one back to examine the stigma attached to the underside. The true petals are the three drooping ones beneath. Bumblebees pollinate iris flowers by pushing between a style and a petal to get at nectar stored deep inside the flower. In doing so, they contact both the anthers and the stigma, and rub pollen onto the latter. Hummingbirds frequently probe for nectar at the base of the petals, bypassing the "correct" route followed by bees. Hummingbirds are nectar thieves of Rocky Mountain iris, since they take nectar without pollinating the flowers in return. Rocky Mountain iris grows in moist meadows and banks throughout the West.

Iris missouriensis Nutt.
Iris Family

97·PALMER LUPINE

Palmer lupine honors Edward Palmer, indefatigable collector of plants, animals, coins, Indian pottery, newspaper clippings and chips knocked off historical buildings. Over his career as a plant collector in the Southwest and Mexico from about 1865 to 1910, Palmer garnered approximately 100,000 specimens, about 2,000 of them then unknown to science. Like many plant collectors in those times, Palmer supported himself by selling his plant specimens to museums and botanical institutions. Palmer lupine flowers are characteristic "bee blossoms." Bees like the blue to violet color of the blossoms and only a strong insect such as a bee can work the flower to extract its pollen and nectar. The creamy-colored spot on the uppermost petal turns magenta once a flower has been pollinated, thus alerting potential pollinators not to waste their time on depleted blossoms. Palmer lupine, a perennial herb, grows in New Mexico and Arizona on roadside banks and in woodland clearings. It blooms in spring and again in summer.

Lupinus palmeri Wats.
Pea Family

98·BLUE FLAX

Blue flax was named *Linum lewisii* after Meriwether Lewis, who discovered it in the Rocky Mountains on his historic expedition of 1804 to 1806. The beautiful bitterroot (*Lewisia rediviva* Pursh), state flower of Montana, was also named in his honor. (Lewis's companion, William Clark, is commemorated in *Clarkia* and other plants.) Although Lewis had no formal training in biology, he did have a discerning eye and the benefit of a crash course in natural history shortly before the expedition. The hundreds of plant specimens he collected on the westward leg of their journey across the Rockies to the Pacific Coast were unfortunately lost in the Missouri River near Great Falls, Montana. On the more hurried return trip, Lewis made a smaller collection of plants, blue flax among them. A relative of cultivated flax, which is native to Europe, blue flax is native to western North America and can be found on slopes and plains from Saskatchewan and Alaska to northern Mexico.

Linum lewisii Pursh
Flax Family

John Richardson

99·ERYNGO

A striking perennial herb, eryngo hardly looks like a relative of the humble dill, yet it is. Most flowers in the Parsley Family, to which both eryngo and dill belong, are borne in umbels, inflorescences that resemble the spokes of an upside-down umbrella. In eryngo, the umbel has collapsed into a flowering head containing dozens of blue flowers with hardly noticeable petals. The white bracts that skirt the flower head take over the function of petals – attracting pollinators. Eryngo grows along roadsides and ditches from west Texas to southeastern Arizona and Mexico. It flowers in the summer.

Eryngium heterophyllum Engelm.
Parsley Family

100·MEXICAN MORNING GLORY

The great Swedish botanist Linnaeus, also known as Carl von Linné, invented a kind of flower sundial which told time according to the opening of various flowers. A southwestern flower clock could start the day with Mexican morning glory: its blue to lavender flowers open at daybreak and close just four or five hours later. Of course, flowers don't coordinate their movements according to human clocks. Dawn or dusk acts as the stimulus for most flowers, which open a certain number of hours after first or last light. By opening for only a few hours early in the day, Mexican morning glory flowers encourage bees (which have a well-developed sense of time) to arrive faithfully for nectar and pollen. Mexican morning glory, a summer-blooming wildflower, twines on trees and shrubs along roadsides and in woodland clearings. It occurs from western Texas to Arizona and to Central America.

Ipomoea hirsutula Jacq. f.
Morning Glory Family

SUGGESTED READING

No guide book can include every wildflower in an area as rich in plant species as the Southwest. You may want to supplement this book with other wildflower identification guides, including:

Arnberger, L. P. *Flowers of the Southwest Mountains*. Tucson: Southwest Parks and Monuments Association, 1982.

Dodge, N. N. *Flowers of the Southwest Deserts*. Tucson: Southwest Parks and Monuments Association, 1985.

Elmore, F. H. *Shrubs and Trees of the Southwest Uplands*. Tucson: Southwest Parks and Monuments Association, 1976.

Martin, W. C. and C. R. Hutchins. *Spring Wildflowers of New Mexico*. Albuquerque: University of New Mexico Press, 1984.

Martin, W. C. and C. R. Hutchins. *Summer Wildflowers of New Mexico*. Albuquerque: University of New Mexico Press, 1986.

Niehaus, T. F. *A Field Guide to Southwestern and Texas Wildflowers*. Boston: Houghton Mifflin Co., 1984.

Phillips, A. M. III. *Grand Canyon Wildflowers*. Grand Canyon: Grand Canyon Natural History Association, 1979.

Readers with some training in botany will find the following manuals indispensible for identifying Southwest wildflowers:

Benson, L. *The Cacti of Arizona*. Rev., 3rd ed. Tucson: University of Arizona Press, 1977.

Benson, L. *The Cacti of the United States and Canada*. Stanford: Stanford University Press, 1982.

Benson, L. and R. A. Darrow. *Trees and Shrubs of the Southwestern Deserts*. 3rd ed. Tucson: University of Arizona Press, 1981.

Kearney, T. H. and R. H. Peebles. *Arizona Flora*. 2nd ed., with supplement by J. T. Howell, E. McClintock and others. Berkeley: University of California Press, 1960.

Martin, W. C. and C. R. Hutchins. *A Flora of New Mexico*. 2 vols. Monticello: J. Cramer, 1980.

Shreve, F. and I. L. Wiggins. *Vegetation and Flora of the Sonoran Desert*. 2 vols. Stanford: Stanford University Press, 1964.

Of the many guides available for identifying insects and birds associated with Southwest wildflowers, I have found the following particularly useful:

Arnett, R. H., Jr. and R. L. Jacques, Jr. *Simon and Schuster's Guide to Insects*. New York: Simon and Schuster, 1981.

Johnsgard, P. A. *The Hummingbirds of North America*. Washington, D. C.: Smithsonian Institution Press, 1983.

Peterson, R. T. *A Field Guide to the Western Birds*. 2nd ed. Boston: Houghton Mifflin, 1961.

Pyle, R. M. *The Audubon Society Field Guide to North American Butterflies*. New York: Alfred A. Knopf, 1981.

Readers who want to learn more about Southwest habitats might find the following books of interest:

Bowers, J. E. *Seasons of the Wind: A Naturalist's Look at the Plant Life of Southwestern Sand Dunes*. Flagstaff: Northland Press, 1986.

Gehlbach, F. R. *Mountain Islands and Desert Seas: A Natural History of the U. S. – Mexican Borderlands*. College Station: Texas A & M University Press, 1981.

Jaeger, E. C. *The North American Deserts*. Stanford: Stanford University Press, 1957.

Kirk, R. *Desert: The American Southwest*. Boston: Houghton Mifflin Co., 1973.

Nabhan, G. P. *Saguaro: A View of Saguaro National Monument and the Tucson Basin*. Tucson: Southwest Parks and Monuments Association, 1986.

A more technical approach to Southwest habitats is taken by the authors of the following books, but the layperson should be able to find much of value in them:

Brown, D. E., ed. *Biotic Communities of the American Southwest – United States and Mexico. Desert Plants* 4: 1-132. Superior: Boyce Thompson Southwestern Arboretum, 1982.

Hastings, J. R. and R. M. Turner. *The Changing Mile*. Tucson: University of Arizona Press, 1965.

McGinnies, W. G. *Discovering the Desert*. Tucson: University of Arizona Press, 1981.

Neither the author nor the publisher endorse the use of any medicinal or edible wild plant discussed in this book. Readers seeking further information on beneficial plants of the Southwest might enjoy:

Moore, M. *Medicinal Plants of the Mountain West*. Santa Fe: Museum of New Mexico Press, 1979.

Nabhan, G. P. *Gathering the Desert*. Tucson: University of Arizona Press, 1985.

INDEX

ACKNOWLEDGMENTS

One Hundred Roadside Wildflowers of Southwest Woodlands is based on numerous articles in scientific journals, too many, unfortunately, to cite each one individually. Without the work of these many scientists, however, I could not have written this book. I also thank Steven P. McLaughlin, Stephen L. Buchmann and Betty Fink, who read the manuscript and contributed ideas and comments.